Your Miracle Source

God's Supernatural Supply for Your Every Need

by

Marilyn Hickey

HARRISON HOUSE
Tulsa, Oklahoma

Unless otherwise indicated, all Scripture quotations are taken from the *King James Version* of the Bible.

06 05 04 03   10 9 8 7 6 5 4 3

Your Miracle Source—
God's Supernatural Supply for Your Every Need
ISBN 1-57794-515-8
(Formerly ISBN 0-89274-240-2)
Copyright © 1982, 2002 by Marilyn Hickey
P.O. Box 17340
Denver, CO 80217

Published by Harrison House, Inc.
P.O. Box 35035
Tulsa, Oklahoma 74153

Contents

1

Husbands Who Believe

In recent years, the world has been in an alarming state of affairs. Is there any hope in such times of need? What does the Bible say? Does God's Word make provision? Does God meet our urgent needs instantaneously? Let us explore. Let us reminisce.

In the past, I was a novice at proving God's Word in times of financial need. I believed in other miracles—miracles of salvation, deliverance, healing, and such—but I had not yet understood that God also intends monetary prosperity for His loved ones.

It was Wally, my husband, who had prior experiences in this "miracle area." He first introduced me to this side of God's dispensation of plenty. It proved to be the beginning of a rude awakening into pleasant green pastures of faith, living with our cup running over.

In the early months of our ministry we were conducting revival meetings in the Colorado area. Between two of the revival meetings we had made a brief stop at home to refresh ourselves. I had no money with me, but I knew Wally was carrying our last $6.50 in his wallet. I had resolved that this should cover the $5 needed for gas, leaving $1.50 for lunch.

After freshening up, I suggested lunch on our way to the next meeting at Glenwood Springs. It was then that the rude shock jolted me. Wally said he had dropped a five-dollar bill in the offering at the previous meeting!

I was dismayed, hungry, and not very willing to settle for a peanut butter and jelly sandwich, but I couldn't argue over his decision to leave an offering. Under my breath I muttered my disappointment at his over-generosity and lack of better management of our money.

Wally, on the other hand, was not one bit flustered. He said, "Let's go by faith. The Lord will provide." We did, despite my discomfort about it. We made a brief stop at my mother's before going on to Glenwood Springs. I was almost tempted to borrow money from her, but I knew Wally wouldn't hear of it. Also, that wouldn't be "trusting in the Lord" for our urgent needs. I determined to believe against unbelief. Needless to say, the Lord came through in a spectacular way, just to make my first experience of His dispensation of plenty more meaningful.

A friend and neighbor of ours, who knew nothing of our circumstances, was quickened by the Holy Spirit of our immediate need. She drove across the city to my mother's and handed us $10. That was double the $5 Wally had placed in the offering!

All our friend said was, "The Lord urged me to get here fast and give you this." To this day, I don't know (and yet I do) how she knew we would stop at our mother's on our way to Glenwood Springs, and even more than that, the exact timing of her trip to meet us.

"Wow!" I reflected. "What a mindful and mysterious God." Our need wasn't big, but it was urgent. He met just that specific requirement. He came through *immediately*.

The second impressive miracle happened shortly afterwards. Wally, seemingly, was totally inconsiderate of our financial situation. This time he dropped a $1,000 check into the offering bag. I didn't try to hide my annoyance at Wally's action. We had so many necessities, like a new car to replace the battered one that threatened to die on us any day.

The first time was a small amount. I could afford to go on faith; but this was different. Just like that he had given away $1,000—months of savings for a new car. "God doesn't need our money," I reasoned. "It's we who are poor."

My first experience had taught me some faith in expecting financial miracles from the Lord, but I hadn't yet learned to believe daringly for God's plenty and to rely on Him entirely.

Wally was patient with me. He had full faith in God's provisions. Soon his calm trust rubbed off on me and I began to trust also, only it was more a resting in the Lord to provide than an immediate expecting.

Six months had passed when an evangelist visited our church. Though he knew nothing of our needs, suddenly in the middle of one of the services, he felt led of the Lord to take an offering for a new car for us.

"Wally, I see the letters 'c-a-r' flashing before me above your head. Do you need a new car?"

Without even consulting Wally, he called on the ushers to take an offering for us, the second offering of the service. Before I could even begin to be startled, the offering was taken. When the money was counted there was more than $1,800. I was choking with tears and could only whisper, "Thank You, Lord Jesus; thank You immensely."

The Lord didn't stop at that. The sale of our old car, which had held together to the last amidst precarious mechanical flaws, provided another $300. This created a total of $2,100 towards a new car!

The Lord had indeed blessed us more than "double portion" this time. I had first experienced the Lord of the "immediate" need. Now I had a taste of the Lord of "plenty." My faith in this whole new miracle area blossomed. I dared to believe Him in the big necessities just as much as in the little ones. I began to trust Him for immediate financial needs, as much as to rest in Him with our entire finances.

Many more personal financial miracles began to pour in. "...precept upon precept, precept upon precept; line upon line, line upon line; here a little, and there a little..." (Isa. 28:13). He allowed me to partake of His promises, to claim His every Word at all times and receive all the provisions that go with them. Personally, I had come a long way, and I was ready for new avenue of this financial adventure with Jesus.

My third phenomenal experience with "the Lord of Finances" unfolded in something more adventurous than I had ever experienced before in my personal life. I dared to launch out in a new ministry for the Lord—on my own, with very little capital. I could not believe that I was really prepared and ready to go this far, but the Lord did. He was bearing me on His wings to new heights and broader horizons!

The "Life For Laymen" radio ministry was born with a meager $60 budget and scriptural promises. With a few devoted pioneers I began the ministry, clinging to those promises in the bag much more dearly than the measly dollars in the cash box. We proceeded in faith.

In just six months the budget increased to $3,000 a month and moved into an additional outreach ministry on television. Our eyes continued to be fixed on the Word and not on the bank account.

Over the years of this ministry, prosperity has rained from "the windows of heaven" because we have leaned wholly on Jesus, the Source of all plenty, and not on our meager financial budget and limited cash with which we had begun. The budget has multiplied beyond recognition of the original amount. Isaiah 28:13 has repeated itself refreshingly!

Experience has been a good teacher. It has led me to new avenues and has proved the Word! Jesus is the Lord of the "immediate." He is the Lord of "double portion." He rains plenty from the windows of heaven on those who will trust and rest on His Word.

2

The Tale of Two Trees

In the beginning chapters of Genesis you will find the original provisions God had made in times of need. Further study will illustrate God's provisions in the contrast between two trees.

There were two trees in the Garden of Eden. One was a beautiful tree, very productive, called the tree of knowledge of good and evil:

> **And out of the ground made the Lord God to grow every tree that is pleasant to the sight, and good for food; the tree of life also in the midst of the garden, and the tree of knowledge of good and evil.**
>
> **Genesis 2:9**

This Scripture indicates that the tree had food upon it, that it was pleasant to the eyes, and that Adam and Eve liked the tree. Every time they looked upon this tree of knowledge of good and evil, the tree looked beautiful. It was very enticing and bore luscious-looking fruit.

However, Adam and Eve were not supposed to eat the fruit of that tree.

> **But of the tree of the knowledge of good and evil, thou shalt not eat of it: for in the day that thou eatest thereof thou shalt surely die.**
>
> **Genesis 2:17**

God gave a very strong command. He said, "Don't eat of that tree!"

But Satan came along and did everything he could to get the woman to eat of that tree.

> **Now the serpent was more subtle than any beast of the field which the Lord God had made. And he said unto the woman, Yea, hath God said, Ye shall not eat of every tree of the garden?**
>
> **Genesis 3:1**

It is Satan's scheming mind that puts questions in God's Word. Did God *really* say what was recorded in Genesis 3:1? Does God *really* mean He wants to heal you? Does God *really* mean He wants to make financial provisions for you, or does He want you to be poor?

If we begin to put question marks on God's Word, we can be assured that it is a result of Satan's instigation.

> **And the woman said unto the serpent, We may eat of the fruit of the trees of the garden: but of the fruit of the tree which is in the midst of the garden, God hath said, Ye shall not eat of it, neither shall ye touch it, lest ye die.**
>
> **Genesis 3:2,3**

But the devil completely negated what God had said to Eve.

> **And the serpent said unto the woman, Ye shall not surely die: for God doth know that in the day ye eat thereof, then your eyes shall be**

opened, and ye shall be as gods, knowing good
and evil.

Genesis 3:4,5

Instead, Satan said, "God doesn't want you to
be as smart as He is, for you may miss something
good." The devil still says that today.

And when the woman saw that the tree was
good for food, and that it was pleasant to the
eyes, and a tree to be desired to make one
wise, she took of the fruit thereof, and did eat,
and gave also unto her husband with her; and
he did eat.

Genesis 3:6

The consequences of partaking that fruit
brought sin and death. God said that if they ate,
they would surely die.

When Adam ate of this tree, he was turned out
of paradise. God put angels with swords east of
the Garden to keep out Adam and Eve so that they
could no longer live in paradise.

The second tree, the tree at Calvary, had to do with Jesus. It was said of Him: "They crucified him, and parted his garments, casting lots: that it might be fulfilled which was spoken by the prophet" (Matt. 27:35).

The cross was a tree as verified by the Scriptures: "The God of our fathers raised up Jesus whom ye slew and hanged on a tree" (Acts 5:30). It is also recalled in Galatians 3:13: "... for it is written, Cursed is every one that hangeth on a tree." When we look at the cross, we must remember God called it a tree.

There are other distinguishing features about the two trees. When Jesus hung upon the cross there was nothing beautiful about the scene; it was bloody.

When Isaiah prophesied about Jesus, he said that Jesus was not pleasant to look at when he hung on the cross: "... he hath no form nor comeliness;

and when we shall see him, there is no beauty that we should desire him" (Isa. 53:2).

This was not true, however, before the time of Jesus' crucifixion. The Bible tells us He grew in stature and, evidently, He was an attractive person until He hung on that cross. The tree of Jesus was not pleasant to look at.

Of the first tree God commanded Adam and Eve not to eat of it; but of the second tree God said, "Taste and see that the Lord is good" (Ps. 34:8).

Jesus even told man to drink of His blood and eat of His flesh. "Verily, verily, I say unto you, Except ye eat the flesh of the Son of man, and drink his blood, ye have no life in you. Whoso eateth my flesh, and drinketh my blood, hath eternal life; and I will raise him up at the last day" (John 6:53,54).

God has issued an open invitation to everyone. Satan beguiled man to go against God's command concerning the first tree, but he hinders man from going to the second tree.

Adam and Eve lost life by "eating;" whereas you and I gain life by eating spiritual food from the second tree. Man died by eating, but he can gain new life by eating of the Word of God. Jesus said, "Man shall not live by bread alone, but by every word that proceedeth out of the mouth of God" (Matt. 4:4).

When Adam and Eve ate of the first tree, they were forced to leave paradise. They had acted like thieves, quietly sneaking up to the tree and eating of the fruit that was not theirs. When Jesus hung on that second tree, a thief who was hanging beside Him said, "Lord, remember me when thou comest into thy kingdom. Jesus replied, Today shalt thou be with me in paradise" (Luke 23:42,43).

It is important to realize that this is the only time Jesus alludes to paradise. Adam ate and was turned out of paradise; the thief partook and was taken into paradise.

Jesus on the cross, the second tree, has every provision that we will ever need. When we partake of His every promise, when we eat of His Word and claim it as ours, then we can receive all the promises that go with it.

The next resemblance is unique and important. When Adam and Eve ate of the tree of knowledge of good and evil, they were really in trouble. When we partake of Jesus we receive the knowledge of good and evil. When we have Jesus, He said that His Spirit will lead us into all truth and that He will give us a knowledge of good and evil.

A new Christian is suddenly turned off to the things he once wanted to do. Nobody, not even the pastor, forced him to change; it was Jesus. He no longer desires to do the things he once loved to do. He never desired to read his Bible or seek Christian fellowship, but now he can't resist. He has partaken of the tree of knowledge of good and evil.

One of the most beautiful experiences of being a Christian is that we can receive divine knowledge of good and evil. Sometimes people wonder: *Do I really have that knowledge?*

Let me assure you that we have the mind of Christ. "Let this mind be in you, which was also in Christ Jesus" (Phil. 2:5). All we have to do is claim it. "...Christ Jesus, who of God is made unto us wisdom, and righteousness, and sanctification, and redemption" (1 Cor. 1:30). When we find ourselves lacking, all we have to do is say, "Jesus, I have Your mind. You live in my heart."

When any man lacks wisdom, the Apostle James says he should do one thing: ask. We can partake of that tree. All we have to do is ask.

Both trees are good for food. When Eve ate of the fruit, she found that it was good for food. When we eat of Jesus, we find Him food for the soul. The real secret of the abundant life in Jesus is to constantly partake of Him in fellowship and communication, and to constantly feed on His Word and let it build us up.

3

Idols Stopping God's Provision

Satan must have said to himself, "If I can get the people involved in idolatry, I can keep them away from the truth." An idol is anything that you can put in place of God. In the Old Testament the people made an image with their own hands and said it was God.

God has something to say about images. "...I shall be satisfied, when I awake, with thy likeness" (Ps. 17:15). "Thy likeness" is a translation of the Hebrew word for "image."[1] The image of God is stamped on your heart.

Psalm 39:6 says man walks in *a vain shew,*[2] which in Hebrew is an "image." Man will walk in an image of what he wants to be or of what Satan has prompted him to be.

Society says a self-made man is one who has lifted himself up by his own bootstraps. He is trying to make himself a success. The Bible tells us that it is not in a man to direct his own paths. (Prov. 3:6.)

Leviticus 26:1 talks of a graven image, which has to do with the image of imagination. Have you ever had your imagination build images and live in fantasy?

We can pick some easy examples of this among teenagers. A boy smiles at a girl and she invites him to the junior prom, though she doesn't even know his name. He just smiled as he walked down the corridor, and she fantasized. Another girl receives a letter from a boy and she reads between the lines. She is sure he is just crazy about her. Another image.

We can formulate images of God which are not true. First Corinthians 11:7 says, "For a man indeed ought not to cover his head, forasmuch as he is the image and glory of God." In God's plan, anyone who belongs to Jesus has the image of God in his life.

Satan, no doubt, had to confuse this truth. He didn't want man to think that, so he came along and introduced false images. He let the people build idols and focus on money, sex, even a personality, as long as they didn't see the truth. He led them on to vain imaginations and wrong things.

He had them make a tree for an image and worship it. For example, the Book of Second Kings says that the people worshiped groves and that Solomon was involved with groves of trees on a high hill. (v. 17:10.)

These trees symbolized the tree of knowledge of good and evil and the tree of life. They worshiped these trees to receive long life. That was Satan's counterfeit.

One Hebrew word meaning "idol" was *Aven*,[3] which also meant a thing of naught,[4] of nothing, or not amounting to anything. The word *beth* in

Hebrew meant "house,"[5] so *Beth-aven* would mean house of nothing.[6] *El* meant God,[7] so Bethel would mean "house of God."[8]

Hosea 4:15 is a verse which might seem to be a play on words, yet is not: "...come not ye unto Gilgal, neither go'ye up to Bethaven, nor swear, the Lord liveth." Amos 5:5 says, "Bethel shall come to nought." In other words, *Bethel* shall come to *Bethaven*. What does that say? The "house of God" shall come in and take over the "house of nothing."

Some people worry about their enemies hexing them—putting pins in dolls and causing evil spirits to bring harm to them, but the house of God will always overcome the house of nothing. The important thing is to remain in the house of God.

As concerning therefore the eating of those things that are offered in sacrifice unto idols, we know that an idol is nothing in the world, and that there is none other God but one.

1 Corinthians 8:4

If we don't get hung up on idols, we don't have to worry about them.

In Acts 14:15 Paul said, "...We also are men of like passions with you, and preach unto you that ye should turn from these vanities unto the living God." Paul was saying that idols are vain things or vanities.

Paul also said that covetousness is idolatry. (Col. 3:5.) Covetousness is wanting something that somebody else has. Money, houses, success, good clothes—these are some of the common things we could covet, but we could also covet another person's spiritual gifts. These are wrong attitudes in spiritual things, and the Bible says that coveting the possessions of another is idolatry.

We are concerned here with financial things, and it is important that our attitudes in possessing material things do not, in any way, border on covetousness. If our attitude is to have a mink coat like the lady next door, if it is to have bigger things, to get ahead of someone, or to be "top dog" in the group by trampling others in the process, then it is idolatry.

We cannot covet because covetousness brings idolatry into our lives. It takes Jesus out of His rightful position and puts Satan in, where he doesn't belong.

The Bible tells us that Jesus has given us all things freely to enjoy, provided they are in their rightful place. (Rom. 8:32; 1 Tim. 6:17.) The anchor for our financial stability should be in Him, not in ourselves; otherwise, our finances will not be successful. The crucial thing is to look at the right tree—Jesus on the cross.

Let us look at another word for idol: *etseb*. This is an interesting word meaning that which causes labor.[9] In other words, you are working endlessly to make that idol. You have worked so hard, but for all your labor, you don't profit from it.

For example, somebody likes money so much that they work hard for it. Just when they think they have made a lot of money, it somehow is not enough. They had their anchor in the wrong place. The idol of their life had been *etseb*.

Another Hebrew word for idolatry is *shiqquwts,* which means "abomination."[10] (2 Chron. 15:8.) Money in the wrong perspective is an idol, a thing of naught, difficult labor that doesn't profit; and it can be an abomination. It can lead you into Satan's world, and even into rebellion.

We are to switch our eyes from the idol as our source to Jesus. Everything we need is found in Jesus; He is our "all sufficient" supply.

When Adam and Eve lived in the Garden, they did not have to worry about anything. God was their total supply. When Jesus came down to this earth, He became your total supply. The Bible says we are complete in Christ.

In Genesis 3:16 God said to the woman, "I will greatly multiply thy sorrow and thy conception." Jesus carried our grief and sorrow. We don't have to carry them anymore. It is also recorded further down in the same chapter that God said to Adam, "...cursed is the ground for thy sake" (v. 17).

In Genesis 3:19 God decreed, "In the sweat of thy face shalt thou eat bread, till thou return unto the ground; for out of it wast thou taken: for dust thou art, and unto dust shalt thou return." In the Garden of Gethsemane, Jesus sweat great drops of blood. (Luke 22:44.) He took the "sweat" out of life.

So he drove out the man; and he placed at the east of the garden of Eden Cherubims, and a flaming sword which turned every way, to keep the way of the tree of life

Genesis 3:24

This meant they could no longer eat of the tree of life. A sword kept them out of the Garden.

Then, many years later, it was a sword, piercing Jesus' side, that made the way for you and me to have access to the Source again.

If we will focus our gaze entirely upon Jesus, we will find that everything is met in Him. He is our total supply!

4

Famine in the Land

The famines of the Old Testament teach us a great lesson about inflation. They tell of God's great deliverance in times of dire financial stress.

God's provisions for His children are always now. If they were sufficient for the Israelites 6,000 years ago, they can be just as abundant for us today.

In Genesis 41, Pharaoh dreamed and Joseph was called to give the interpretation: "There will be seven years of plenty followed by seven years of famine. Prepare for the seven years of famine and God will meet us there."

Joseph is one of the most beautiful "types of Jesus" in the Old Testament. When Joseph came to Pharaoh and interpreted his dream, Pharaoh was so excited about it that he gave Joseph a new name. He called him, *Zaphnath-paaneah,* meaning "Savior of the world."[1] The name *Joseph* itself meant "He will add."[2] Both the old and the new names of Joseph symbolize something very significant—a truth about Jesus.

Think about the first Adam. The first Adam subtracted, but Jesus, the second Adam, *added* something into people's lives. He is also the Savior of the world.

Pharaoh gave Joseph a bride. (Gen. 41:45.) Her name was Asenath, which tells us that she was a Gentile bride. What about the bride of Jesus? His bride is a Gentile bride, too. The former bride of God was Jewish and for the most part did not accept Jesus, so God gave Jesus a Gentile bride.

Verse 46 says, "Joseph was thirty years old when he stood before Pharaoh king of Egypt." Jesus, too, was thirty years old when He began His public ministry!

Here is another intriguing thought to mull over: Israel became God's own when they were in Egypt. It was because of the Egyptians, who were Gentiles, that they first sacrificed a lamb. Wouldn't it be something if the Jewish revival broke out because the Gentiles brought them the truth again? It looks as though it is going to be so. All signals point that way.

Joseph had two little boys. (Gen. 41:50.) One was Manasseh and the other was Ephraim. We see a parallel to this in Jesus' story also. *Manasseh* meant "causing to forget."[3] When Jesus came, the Jews "forgot" that He was their Messiah. They didn't remember the Scriptures and their eyes were blinded. *Ephraim,* on the other hand, meant "fruitful."[4] When Jesus came, while the Jews "forgot," the Gentiles became "fruitful."

The Gentiles reaped the fruits of the tree of life—Jesus—while the Jews slumbered in oblivious amnesia. There are two parts—one group received and the other rejected.

Joseph's two boys also represent God's past and future dealings with Israel. His past dealings very clearly depict His disappointment in them, while His future dealings promise hope for them. The Jews are "coming" yet. The period of forgetfulness will be followed by a period of fruitfulness.

After seven years of plenty in Egypt, there were seven terrible years of famine. After Jesus walked among the Jews and invited them to come to the Messiah, whom they rejected, they were in the midst of famine. It is a significant parallel which cannot be overlooked. In the Scriptures it is called "Jacob's trouble."

Joseph was a great blessing to the land of Egypt and to his family. He was the provider of bread in time of famine. He gave food to the Egyptians first, and later, when his family came, he gave them bread. He was the dispenser of bread. Some 6,000 years after this story, Jesus was called "the Bread of Life."

Romans 11:11 says, "...through their fall salvation is come unto the Gentiles." Visualize the fate of the Egyptians had Joseph not come to them. Egypt would certainly have starved to death.

When Joseph met his brothers and they recognized him, they became afraid, recalling the wretched thing they had done to him. But Joseph was quick to assure them, "You meant it for evil, but God took it for good." When Jesus was crucified by the Jews, even though they meant it for evil at that time, God took it for their eventual good, another striking parallel.

Another unique similarity that we see in the two stories is the supply that was, and is, unlimited, both in the time of Joseph and today with Jesus. There was, and is, plenty to give, both in the barns of Joseph and in the tree of Jesus. The supply was, and is, limitless.

Joseph was the giver of bread; Jesus is the Bread of Life. Joseph was the source in the time of famine; Jesus is the Source in times of financial need today. Jesus is our Savior in the time of need, as was Joseph to the people of his day.

And there was a famine in the land: and Abram (Abraham) went down into Egypt to sojourn there; for the famine was grievous in the land.

Genesis 12:10

This is the first famine recorded in the Bible. Abraham was called to go to Canaan, the Promised Land. He left part of his family, including his wife, but took with him his father and nephew. When he reached the Promised Land, there was, to his great surprise, famine in the land!

Could there be a famine in spiritual places? How can there be any "need" in God's spiritual grounds? Abraham probably reacted like any of us had we been in his place. He wandered off to Egypt and lived there, for the famine was grievous in the Promised Land.

While he was in Egypt he lied and said that his wife was his half-sister. He picked up some-body in Egypt that he could have left behind—Hagar, a handmaid.

When Abraham brought Hagar home, Sarah, his wife, said, "Why can't you live with Hagar? She can have a child, and we can raise him as ours." That was never God's plan. Abraham spoiled it by listening to Sarah.

Today when we go to "Egypt," we look to the wrong source and reason away what God can do in and out of our circumstances. We should stay in Canaan land and trust God to meet us there in times of famine. Who wants a "Hagar?" Don't reason away the promises of God.

It may seem like good sense to leave Canaan for a little while and go to Egypt, but then we miss

God's provisions by allowing our reason to become the source. It got Abraham, the patriarch of faith, into trouble. We can't afford to repeat the mistake.

There was another famine recorded in Genesis having to do with Isaac.

> **There was a famine in the land, beside the first famine that was in the days of Abraham. And Isaac went unto Abimelech king of the Philistines unto Gerar. And the Lord appeared unto him, and said, Go not down into Egypt.**
>
> **Genesis 26:1,2**

God said unto Isaac, "Don't do what your daddy did." Rather, "...dwell in the land which I shall tell thee of; sojourn in this land, and I will be with thee, and will bless thee; for unto thee, and unto thy seed, I will give all these countries, and I will perform the oath which I sware unto Abraham thy father" (Gen. 26:2,3). Isaac obeyed.

In our present lingo, "Stay put. Don't leave. Listen to Me; I will bless you and bless you until it comes out your ears." Our reasoning could have replied, "Daddy went to Egypt and came back with a lot of money and Mother came back with a new maid. It didn't seem all that bad."

Piercing through our reasoning, however, would be the voice of God, loud and clear, saying, "Don't repeat the mistake of your father. Stay put and I will deliver you."

"God is our refuge and strength, a very present help in trouble" (Ps. 46:1). He is a definite help in times of need, whether it be a famine in the Promised Land of yesterday, or a recession in a comparable land that God has promised to lead us in today. He is our all-time Source.

Scriptures are for our instruction. Experiences of our forefathers are for our guidance. We cannot repeat the mistakes of our fathers and miss God's land of plenty. Abraham's experience is a warning; Isaac's is an example. We must let God be our Source. God blessed Isaac in a big way. Truly, He is our total supply!

We have seen three things that can hinder our receiving answers for financial needs: covetousness, the mistake of idolizing money, and the oft-repeated temptation to reason away what God can do in specific times of financial need.

If you say that you have sensed nothing personally, then you have nothing to worry about. God won't deal with you without first showing it to you clearly. He is not nebulous. He will make His intentions very clear.

You don't say to your children, "I don't know whether you ought to go to bed at 7 or 11." If 9 PM is bedtime, you don't ambiguously whisper it to your children. You are specific in your instructions. God is the same way. He will let you know.

God will deal with us to correct the wrongs in our lives. If He reveals an area of wrong to you, confess it and do your best to get it right.

5

Ravens and Widows

Again, there was a famine in the land of Israel. For three years there had been no rain, only drought upon the land. The people were starving.

God led Elijah into a tiny place by the brook called Cherith. (1 Kings 17:2-7.) He sustained Elijah in a very unusual way in this seemingly "God-forsaken place." God gave him water and sent ravens to bring bread and meat to him twice a day. Elijah had two meals a day in the midst of famine.

Ravens were unclean birds, so Elijah could have legitimately complained, "Wrong kind of birds, God. Send me an eagle." He didn't do that.

God can bring finances to us in such unusual ways that we say, "This way of receiving Your plenty doesn't fit. Wrong way, Lord." Elijah didn't say, "Wrong bird," should you?

Another interesting fact was that the ravens were hungry, too. They could have eaten the meat themselves on their way. God knew how to get the ravens to feed His children and not eat what the children were supposed to have.

There may be "ravens" in your life that are eating what you are supposed to have, but God can take care of those "ravens" so that they supply you without feeding themselves.

While Elijah continued to live a blissful life by the brook, oblivious to the hardships of famine, the brook eventually dried. Sometimes God can meet our needs in a certain way, then change the course on us. At such times we question, "Where is God now?" He is just changing the course of the pipeline so you won't get your eyes on the mailman or on the wealthy uncle or on that philanthropic friend. He can change the type of His dispensation.

God said to Elijah, "Go to Zarephath; I have prepared a widow to feed you." Zarephath was in Zidon. (v.9.) If I were Elijah I would have said, "Not Zarephath, Lord. You know what Zarephath is. That's Jezebel's hometown!"

Jezebel hated Elijah. The last time they had met she said, "If it's the last thing I do, I'll kill you!" Now of all places, God sent Elijah to Jezebel's hometown. What was God doing to Elijah? He was getting his eyes away from the problem and bringing him to a total dependence on the total Source—Himself.

Then God said, "I have a widow to sustain thee." But that didn't sound very promising either. Why couldn't God pick somebody more appropriate? However, Elijah obeyed God and went to Zarephath.

When he came to the gates of the city, there was the widow woman gathering some sticks. (A rich widow couldn't be doing that!) Elijah called her and said, "Fetch me, I pray thee, a little water in a vessel, that I may drink" (v. 10).

As she went to bring it, Elijah called after her and said, "Bring me, I pray thee, a morsel of bread in thine hand" (v. 11).

Her reply to Elijah was even more astounding: "As the Lord thy God liveth, I have not a cake, but an handful of meal in a barrel, and a little oil in a cruse: and, behold, I am gathering two sticks, that I may go in and dress it for me and my son, that we may eat it, and die" (v. 12).

A dying widow woman was to sustain a prophet of God? God couldn't be that blind! Elijah was in a spot: On the one hand, there were the perils of death due to starvation; on the other hand, there was a wicked woman hunting for his blood. Even the strangest fiction can't beat this story!

This certainly doesn't sound to me like good provision from the Lord. Elijah replied to her with a confidence that matched the provision: "Fear not; go and do as thou hast said: but make me thereof a little cake first, and bring it unto me, and after make for thee and for thy son" (v. 13).

The Bible tells us that under all circumstances we have to bring our first-fruits unto God. You may say, "But I can't afford it." Do you think this widow woman could afford to feed Elijah first? Certainly not. Don't ever let your reasoning take you out of faith.

This widow was really providing for her children by her faith. This was her test to look to God as her source. Elijah continued, "For thus saith the Lord God of Israel, The barrel of meal shall not waste, neither shall the cruse of oil fail, until the day that the Lord sendeth rain upon the earth" (v. 14). There was something else that was interesting in this story: the supply did not last throughout the whole famine. It lasted maybe two and a half years, just until the rain started. When the rain started, the meal barrel and the cruse of oil stopped supplying and they had to go to work.

We may say, "I will have faith and sit and wait for God to bring it in." God isn't making lazy people out of us by putting us on spiritual welfare. That is not His way of providing for us. Faith is very active.

Miracles take us through only what we cannot do, not what we can do. Miracles are for a real time of desperation. Once that time is over, the Bible says that the man who doesn't work, doesn't eat. (2 Thess. 3:10.) It's that simple. God prospers what we do. When there was a famine in the land, God made provisions for a woman who was willing to take the last bits she had and give it to God's work.

When such clamps are on, many of us say, "I'm going to cut my giving." By doing that we cut off our Source. If faith had been reasonable, Elijah would not have gone to Zarephath. If faith had been rationalized, the widow woman would not have obeyed. But she obeyed.

Let's see what happened. "And she went and did according to the saying of Elijah: and she, and he, and her house, did eat many days" (v. 15).

God has such strange ways of meeting us. Don't ever try to reason out how He is going to do it. He has many ways in which to work His wonders. Trust Him.

In one of our miracle services we gathered around to pray over our billfolds, but no one prayed over his own. In such giving in prayer, they received. Many called in after the miracle service and testified to the financial blessings they had received. One man called to say that he received a large raise. Another found a lucrative job. Many good things began to happen because God was becoming the Source in their lives.

The supply of meal and oil did not fail the whole time Elijah lived there. God was taking care of all three of them—Elijah, the widow, and her son. God performs His miracles in unique, unusual, and sometimes unreasonable ways.

It is God's will for us to prosper. Something fantastic and unique can be found in Isaiah 48:15. Here God does not say you will be prosperous, but that He will make your *way* prosperous.

It is important that you be constantly aware of the Source, and not the supply. God's ways are above our ways. (Isa. 55:9.) He is the total supplier of all our needs!

6

Feed Your Enemies

Second Kings, chapter 6, narrates another peculiar miracle of God. We know that God loves His children; therefore, He really loves you. When you love your children, you never want them to go hungry. In fact, you probably stuff them with food every chance you get!

God is concerned about you even more than you are about your children. In this miracle God feeds an army of the enemy's camp instead of His children. We will not go into all the details of this story, only the essential lesson that we may draw from it.

The Syrian army came to fight the Israelites. They were mad because Elisha, the man of God, was giving away all their military secrets. They were after his blood. First, they came down and surrounded the little town of Dothan, where Elisha lived. Dothan means "double feast," so this name fits the town where a miracle was later performed.

While the armies surrounded Elisha's town, the servant of Elisha spotted them and was panic-stricken. He cried to Elisha, "Did you see? I just raised the blinds and saw the whole Syrian army surrounding us. What is to become of us now?"

Elisha prayed, "God, raise the blinds on the eyes of my servant."

When the servant was enlightened, he cried even louder and said, "Now I see the Lord round-about the place, and I see chariots of fire!"

Then Elisha prayed another prayer. He said, "God, blind the eyes of the enemy," and God did. When the enemy came walking into town, they could not find their way and were confused. They walked straight into Elisha and, not knowing who he was, asked him where they could find Elisha.

Elisha said, "Come with me," and he led them right to the king of Israel. That was a seventeen-mile march! When they got to the king of Israel, Elisha said, "God, open their eyes now."

How ridiculous they must have felt when they realized what had happened. They raised a cry, but to no avail. They screamed, "That was not at all what we meant. We wanted to be led to Elisha, not to the king!"

The king of Israel wanted to kill them, but Elisha said, "Don't kill them; feed them!" Jesus said to feed your enemies; be good to them; bless them. So the king of Israel fed the whole Syrian army, and they went home, never to bother the Israelites again.

Out of His goodness, God leads people to repentance. For the sake of leading a soul to surrender,

God will even provide food for them. His provisions include even the people in the enemy's camp. He is a total supplier!

Second Kings, chapter 7, tells another strange story about the real price of inflation of that time. If you think that inflation in our times is bad, you need to read this story. Today's needs are nothing compared to the atrocious prices of Elisha's time.

Then Elisha said, Hear ye the word of the Lord; Thus saith the Lord, To morrow about this time shall a measure of fine flour be sold for a shekel, and two measures of barley for a shekel.

2 Kings 7:1

That must have been the craziest statement of that day. There was a famine in the land, and the most incredible and worthless food items cost a fortune.

In chapter 6, verse 25, it tells us that for fourscore pieces of silver you could buy an ass's head. That equals $51.20 in our money. A fourth of a dove's dung could be bought for five pieces of silver, or

$3.20. Dove's dung wasn't literally that, but a type of grain that was fed to the dove.

If that wasn't an *inflated* inflation, how else could you describe it? I would say that the inflation of our day and age would be chicken feed compared to those days of dove's food and donkey's heads!

Elisha came into this situation and, with a calm, cool audacity, announced that everything was going to change the very next day. Can you imagine how furious that would have made a starving, hungry mob of people?

Do you know how fast God can change things? "Some day," you say, "God will give me these things. Maybe next month or next year when I am retiring. He will make me comfortable."

But do you know that it could be the following day? In Elisha's time, God brought inflation down in just one day. God is the same today. His power hasn't diminished with usage over the years, nor is His concern any less for us today.

Elisha said, *"By this time tomorrow,* flour will be a penny and two measures of barley will be a penny."

The irritation of a majority of the people at this statement showed forth in one man—the king's servant. "Never can that be. It is preposterous!" he shouted.

Elisha said, "Don't believe it now, but you will see it with your own eyes and never be able to eat it." The whole story is the most extraordinary one I have ever read. *God used four lepers.* Four lepers who were starving to death along with the rest of the people. They were saying, "What shall we do? Shall we leave the city, or shall we stay here and die? For we will die either way." They decided to go out to the Syrian army at twilight.

The Bible tells us that God caused the Syrian army to hear a noise. You saw how God can close eyes, but He can also cause people to hear strange things. In one place it was the eyes, in another it was the ears that played tricks on the Syrian army. Believing that another army was coming after them, they ran!

When the four lepers arrived on the scene, they didn't know what was going on. They walked into the Syrian tents and found an abundance of delicious food. They sat down before that fabulous table of all those delectable goodies and ate and ate. The clothes they tried on were just their size. They ate and drank, and ate and drank again!

When they were finally exhausted with eating and drinking, they said, "Maybe we should go back and tell the king." The lepers returned and told the man at the gate. He ran to the palace and woke the king in the middle of the night to retell their story. Of course, the king was skeptical, proclaiming, "I'm sure it's a trap. It *has* to be a trap!"

He dispatched a handful of his men. They looked around very cautiously. They had to be careful for they had only four horses left. All the rest had been eaten during the famine. The soldiers discovered that the Syrian army was gone, and all their food and enormous wealth had been left behind. They couldn't believe their eyes, nor could they understand why the Syrian army left without their possessions. It was a huge army and their supplies were plenty.

In the face of such plenty nobody questioned why this much food was left behind, nor did they waste a thought wondering who could have frightened them away. A hungry mob of soldiers and civilians alike went crazy, clamoring to get at the food.

The next day the soldiers brought all the goods into the city and sold them at the gates. The people were buying barley and flour for practically nothing. Inflation was a thing of the past. Prosperity had boomed overnight!

The king's servant exclaimed, "This could never be unless God had opened the windows of heaven." God did—He had opened the lepers' eyes. When the eyes of those four hungry lepers were opened and they found all that food, they became the heavenly angels of good tidings to a starving, famine-stricken crowd of people.

Like everybody else, the servant of the king saw the plenty and raced to the gates of the city to get his share. But the people stepped on him before he could reach the food and he died in the stampede. His ears heard Elisha's prophecy, but his heart refused to believe. His eyes saw the prophecy come true, but his belly couldn't be satisfied with the food and he died while reaching for it.

Unbelief can cause you to die while everybody else is getting their provision. If you want to live, believe in the Source, or else you will die in unbelief. When you do not believe in Jesus as your Source, then you will die in spiritual poverty. God can open your windows in this most unique way. Believe Him!

When God's channels flow, the very windows of heaven will open. Deflate inflation by centering on the true economic Source—Jesus Christ!

7

Behind Closed Doors

Let us look at the story of another widow in 2 Kings, chapter 4. God takes the worst cases to show us that it doesn't really matter how bad the situation is. We tend to say, "Their case isn't as bad as mine," so God says, "I will show you the worst."

This is a particularly great and interesting miracle because it involves a family. When you study miracles in the lives of Elisha, Elijah, and Jesus, you will see that a number of their miracles have to do with family life. This is where we need miracles the most.

Now there cried a certain woman of the wives of the sons of the prophets unto Elisha,

saying, Thy servant my husband is dead; and thou knowest that thy servant did fear the Lord: and the creditor is come to take unto him my two sons to be bondmen.

2 Kings 4:1

Here was a woman in desperation. Yet the Scriptures don't emphasize that. They simply state that she cried. Looking into her background, I noticed that there was something interesting about her husband. Here she said to Elisha, "Your servant, my husband." Undoubtedly, her husband must have gone through the school of prophets under Elisha and Elijah. It was the well-known school for prophets in those days.

Many Bible scholars believe, and I agree, that the man, who was the dead husband of this widow, was Obadiah. Obadiah, you might recall, was the one who hid the hundred prophets and fed them from Jezebel's table.

When the widow said, "Your servant feared the Lord," she was talking of someone who truly feared the Lord, one who was willing to risk even his life to feed the prophets of God. Here lies a nugget of golden truth we cannot overlook. If we fear the Lord and remain faithful to Him in our sphere of activity, He will honor us and our families. We can be sure that when we make a stand for God on His Word, it will always be rewarded. It is absolutely impossible for the Word of God to return void. (Isa. 55:11.)

The widow cried because she was in desperate need of help from the man of God. She presented the best line of argument that she knew. She pleaded with the prophet on the strength of her husband. She was making a case for herself and she could not have chosen a better line, "My husband was a godly man!"

This is a good basis of approach unto the throne of grace today when we find ourselves in a similarly bad situation. "Lord, my household and my forefathers have always feared thee." The Lord cannot help but honor that kind of stand, for He

has promised blessings unto a thousand genera-
tions of them that fear and love Him. (Ex. 20:5,6.)

Because Obadiah had passed away, his poor
wife and her two sons were without any money
and without a breadwinner to take care of them.
The creditors were after them to take the sons
away to be their bondsmen, as was the custom of
those days.

When somebody owed a debt and could not
pay, they had to give their sons, not to be slaves
for life, but to serve the creditors for a specific
time period in lieu of the unpaid debt. It was the
law of the land that God had set up in Leviticus.

However, this widow did not become dismayed, even in the face of such perilous threats.
Instead, she remembered the man of God under
whom her husband had served the Lord. She cried
out loudly.

It might seem strange to you, as it did to me,
that the story talks about only one widow who

cried out. There must have been other widows in similar hardships, but only this woman cried out to make known that she was in dire need. Also, she obviously knew to whom she should go in seeking help. She released her faith.

This story can be looked at in three ways. First, there is always a connection to a miracle. There will always be some little link—somebody who will be God's connection to unfold the miracle. The widow's connection was Elisha. *Elisha* means "God is salvation." The widow probably said to herself, "I am going to the one who knows that God can bring deliverance (salvation) and I am going to seek him out," and she did.

As a pastor friend of ours was traveling to a fellowship meeting, he ran into a snowstorm. The roads were icy, and his car was not equipped with snow tires. As he drove down the highway he spotted a man whose jeep had run into a ditch. When our friend offered to pull him out of the ditch, the man asked if he had snow tires. Of course he didn't, but he had the Lord on his side. He assured the man that he could handle it.

He hooked his car to the jeep then carefully pulled it out onto the highway and then to a filling station. Amazed, the man got out and said, "I want to thank you for what you have done." Then he bought our friend two snow tires, pulled out his billfold, gave him two $100 bills, and drove off. There are always connections, sometimes divine connections, to miracles!

The second point of this story has to do with receivers of miracles. Anyone who has a need can receive miracles. The woman who came to Elisha had a real need. As a widow, she had no one to take care of her. If her two sons should leave to pay the debt, then the woman would, in all probability, starve to death. She said, "I have to have a miracle; there is no way out. My only connection is Elisha."

It was good that she went to Elisha. That was the right thing to do. But the reaction of the prophet was far from what you would have expected. "And Elisha said unto her, what shall I do for thee? tell me, what hast thou in the house?" (v. 2).

Let's assume that you came to me and said, "Marilyn, I need to borrow a hundred dollars from you."

If I should reply, "What do you want me to do about it?" how would you react?

If I had said, "What do you have in the house? Got any leftovers in the refrigerator?" what would you have done? Your thoughts might have been: "Look, I'm asking *you* for help. Don't ask me if I have anything to use."

There are some key points in this miracle. Elisha did not do one active thing. He just turned around and asked her two questions: "What am I supposed to do?" and "What do you have in the house?"

She replied sweetly, "Your handmaid has nothing in the house, except a pot of oil."

Notice what he said, "Go and borrow all the empty vessels you can get from your neighbors. Don't take just a few, but a lot." The real test of this miracle is right now.

Suppose that when you came to me to borrow the hundred dollars, I had said, "Why don't you borrow from somebody else?" Certainly that would not have sounded good to you.

When looking on the map, I found that this widow lived in the northern part of Israel near Zidon, the tiny area where the tribe of Asher lived. The Scriptures say that Asher would dip his foot in oil. (Deut. 33:24.) I am sure that at the time of this story there were olive trees in this area, for God had prophesied through Moses that the tribe of Asher would live where there were many olive trees. Their main source was probably oil.

This widow woman was living in that area; yet she was going out to borrow *empty* vessels. I suspect that everybody needed a miracle, that the entire city was in financial distress and everyone had empty pots.

The economy may be tight today, but our times are not nearly as bad as those. We don't know anything about famine in this country. Even if 8% of our people are out of work, the remaining 92% are still working. At the time of this Bible story, apparently 100% were unemployed, for *all* their vessels were empty!

Then he told her the strangest thing of all. "When you get home, close the door upon you and your two sons; then you pour into all these vessels. When they are full, set them aside."

She would have to borrow a lot of empty vessels because faith is active, never passive. It always involves action. To prove the negative of this, let me share a comical story about my husband's great-uncle who lived next door when my husband was a boy. Day after day, this man would sit in his rocking chair on the front porch, rocking back and forth, and rhythmically repeat, "I wish I had a million dollars." Do you think he ever got that million dollars? You are right—he didn't.

There are Christians who say, "I wish I had a miracle." But they will never get it until they *act* on the Word.

This widow had to borrow empty vessels. You may think, "What am I going to do with all those empty pots and pans?"

Look at the crucial point of the miracle mentioned earlier. This story involved the whole family. God always wants the whole family unit involved when He performs a miracle. I wonder how her two sons felt about these things. They certainly were involved in this miracle. It was the sons who went out to borrow the vessels from their neighbors. They were probably like my children, who hated to borrow even a cup of sugar for me. However, they knocked at every door in the neighborhood and brought back empty vessels.

The mother's role in this miracle was her activity. She did the pouring. Elisha didn't do it. The sons didn't do it. It takes big faith to act foolishly. Here she was with all those big vessels and just a puny jar of oil—and she had to pour. Elisha, the man of God, told her to do it, so she did!

She left Elisha, shut the door behind herself and her sons, told them to bring the vessels to her, and started pouring. The oil just kept coming. When one vessel was full, she moved to the next. She poured and poured, and finally said, "Bring me yet another vessel." When her son answered, "There are no more vessels," the flow of oil stopped.

Your faith will extend as far as your actions. When the supply of vessels stopped, the supply of oil stopped, too. If there had been more vessels, there would have been more oil.

She then told the man of God. His reply was, "Go, sell the oil, and pay thy debt, and live thou and thy children of the rest" (v. 7). Not only was there enough to pay the debt, there was also enough to live on. The Bible doesn't say how long it lasted, but I suspect it lasted until the famine was over.

Some say they retired on that income, but I think not. The supply lasts only for the time of need. When conditions return to normal, God's miraculous flow ceases and man's natural effort begins once again.

Now, let us look into the requirements of the miracle: Close the door; pour into the vessels; set aside that which is full.

Why did Elisha say, "Shut the door upon thee and upon thy sons?" (v. 4.) There was a good reason for this: to keep out the doubters. Recall the time in Mark, chapter 5, when Jesus healed Jairus' daughter. Jesus put out all the mourners and closed the door. Only Jesus stayed inside. Peter, James, John, and the parents of the damsel were believers, but Jesus was routing out unbelief.

One of the secrets of getting a miracle is closing the door on unbelief in yourself and others. Peter did it also when he raised a woman who was dead. (Acts 9:36-41.) He prayed for her in seclusion, away from unbelief, and she was raised from the dead.

The unbelief may not always be your own. It may be that of a loved one, or a neighbor, even that of your pastor. There is a time when you have to close the door on unbelief. It is essential that we take the Word and stand on it and it alone.

Let's not miss another point in our miracle story. When the miracle occurred, it was not Elisha who was present, but the widow and her family. How many times do we say, "If Brother so-and-so had come and prayed, I know my husband or child would have been healed." Elisha put the woman's eyes on the right Source, and away from himself. He was only the connection of the miracle. He only spoke the Word. She was the one acting out the miracle, and God was the Source of the miracle supply. The connection of your miracle is God's Word.

The widow went for advice after the miracle, inquiring of the prophet what she should do with her supply. Many times, when we begin to prosper, we go on a spending spree. We should go to God and ask Him what He wants us to do with it.

She went back to the man of God and asked how she should use the oil. He said, "Sell it and pay your debt; then you and the children can live on the rest of it."

Notice how practical God is. He had her pay off her debts *first,* then live on the rest. Many times we live it up, then try to pay the debts with what is left at the end of the month. That is not God's way.

It is beautiful to note that in the Old Testament, every time they met God in a new way, they gave Him a new name, and vice versa. For example, God appeared to Abram and said, "Abram, I am El Shaddai, and I am going to call you *Abraham* because you are going to be father of many." *El Shaddai* means the many-breasted one, or one who has total nourishment,[1] a whole or total place of supply.

If we had looked at Abram, we would have said, "Abram, you and your wife are too old to have children. There is no way out." But God said, "That is when I become the total supply of what you need."

The name *El Shaddai* is used more times in the Book of Job than any place else. Job said, "God, I don't have anything." Job had lost everything, so it was little wonder then that he addressed God as *El Shaddai.* When Job acknowledged Him thusly, God gave him a double portion.

When I found that Job called God *El Shaddai* more times than anybody else, I said to myself,

"Lord, that must be a mistake. Job couldn't call you *El Shaddai* because he was one of the poor ones."

God said, "Yes, it is the poorest ones who meet God as the total Source of supply."

God's supply of oil is always grace. The widow woman didn't deserve it; she just got it. You don't deserve it; you just need it. She said, "O Lord, I have a need," and He said, "I will bring a miracle supply that will pay the debt and enough will remain to take you through."

It pays to ask for the miraculous in your life. You are not going to have it unless you do. Close the door on unbelief and ask the right Source, the total Source—*El Shaddai!*

8

Five Promises of Prosperity

There are unique scriptural meanings to numbers because they speak God's mathematical language. Three is the number of the Trinity; seven is the perfect number; six is the number of man.

Since five is the number of grace, I decided to look up the number five in the Scriptures:

> **And he (Joseph) took and sent messes (portions) unto them from before him: but Benjamin's mess was FIVE times so much as any of theirs. And they drank, and were merry with him.**
>
> **Genesis 43:34**

> **To all of them he gave each man changes of raiment; but to Benjamin he gave...FIVE changes of raiment.**
>
> **Genesis 45:22**

In this situation, Joseph, who was a type of Christ, showed unmerited favor on Benjamin. God pours forth unmerited favor, too.

Interestingly, the miracle story of the widow's oil multiplied, which we studied in the last chapter, happens to be the *fifth* miracle of Elisha's life.

This *fifth* miracle is a total miracle of grace, of unmerited favor. The widow's miracle continued even after the miracle of the pouring forth because she let it be so. She went back to the man of God, who was her link with the Source, and maintained the relationship with the Source. The secret to her success was in letting God do it— before, during, and after. As far as she was concerned, the provision was totally His.

Many financial problems in our lives today are due to misspending money. Credit cards, for the most part, have been abused. Undue celebrations over interim prosperity have, in many cases, been the cause of ruin. And these misdirections continue because we do not go back to the Source, like this widow did, for guidance in budgeting and in paying our debts.

Basically, grace is "letting Jesus do it." The all-inclusive key to prosperity is Jesus Christ and our letting Him be gracious unto us all the way—from blessing us with prosperity to commanding us to tithe, directing us to pay the debts, helping us budget, and even save it to reinvest but not hoard. It is letting Him handle our financing and our finances. The widow woman did precisely that.

The experiences of these Bible miracles apply to us by appropriating in our lives today their experiences with the total Supplier. God's *today provisions* are for us as His *yesterday supplies* were for those in need then. Jesus is the same yesterday, today, and tomorrow. (Heb. 13:8.) He is the all-time, all-inclusive key to prosperity.

Now you know the Source of your miracle—Jesus. You know the richness of His supply—unlimited. *Try* Him in your current financial struggle (if you have one) and see whether He will finance you. *Taste* the fruits of the tree of life, for they have been proven good. *Turn over* the finances that you are blessed with through the luscious circle of giving and receiving.

Finally, remember the five crucial activities that are involved in this divine monetary flow. Two are His as the Supplier. Three are yours as the receiver. Jesus will open the very windows of heaven if these activities are respected and done. They are in His Word.

1. God wills that we prosper.

Beloved, I wish above all things that thou mayest prosper and be in health, even as thy soul prospereth.

3 John 2

...he (the Lord) shall make his way prosperous.

Isaiah 48:15

74

This is not that we will be prosperous in a stationary condition, but that He will make our way prosperous, implying action. The God of heaven will prosper us; therefore, as His servants we will arise and build.

Angels are involved in prosperity. "The Lord, before whom I walk, will send his angel with thee, and prosper thy way" (Gen. 24:40).

2. We begin to claim prosperity.

Thou hast caused men to ride over our heads; we went through fire and through water: but thou broughtest us out into a wealthy place.

Psalm 66:12

If you are going through fire and water in your financial situation, know that God promises you a wealthy place. Take this Word and stand on it. It is His intention for you to mature in faith!

Riches come many times in the days of famine and persecution. "They shall not be ashamed in the evil time: and in the days of famine they shall be satisfied" (Ps. 37:19).

You may feel that you can't prosper in a time of recession, but did God say that? No. God's Word says, "Behold, the eye of the Lord is upon them that fear him...to deliver their soul from death, and to keep them alive in famine" (Ps. 33:18,19).

We are not to be hung up on money, only on the Supplier of money. "...give me neither poverty nor riches; feed me with food convenient for me: lest I be full, and deny thee, and say, Who is the Lord? or lest I be poor, and steal, and take the name of my God in vain" (Prov. 30:8,9).

3. **When we keep His Word, God will prosper us.**

   Keep therefore the words of this covenant, and do them, that ye may prosper in all that ye do.

   Deuteronomy 29:9

   So shall my word be that goeth forth out of my mouth: it shall not return unto me void, but it

**shall accomplish that which I please, and it
shall prosper in the thing whereto I sent it.**

Isaiah 55:11

**And now, brethren, I commend you to God,
and to the word of his grace, which is able to
build you up, and to give you an inheritance
among all them which are sanctified.**

Acts 20:32

Keeping God's Word is an essential activity
that will cause the very windows of heaven to
gush forth with His prosperity.

4. As we seek Him, God prospers us.

**...as long as he sought the Lord, God made
him to prosper.**

2 Chronicles 26:5

Normally, I don't think we become desperate
about seeking the Lord. Perhaps at night we pray,
"Now I lay me down to sleep...." Then we wake
saying, "Now I'm awake; take care of me today."
We say we have done well during a day if we have
read one psalm. That is not seeking the Lord!

77

> ...who hath hardened himself against him
> (God), and hath prospered?
>
> Job 9:4

You cannot hide from God and prosper for very long; but if you seek Him, He will make your way continually prosperous.

> If ye abide in me, and my words abide in you,
> ye shall ask what ye will, and it shall be done
> unto you.
>
> John 15:7

> He satisfieth the longing soul, and filleth the
> hungry soul with goodness.
>
> Psalm 107:9

Seek God and spend time in His presence. Make your hunger known to Him.

5. The lips of the righteous feed many.

Your prosperity depends on what you say with your mouth. We have seen that it depends on our activities, such as seeking God and keeping His Word. Now God's Word is saying, "Claim the Word."

A man's belly shall be satisfied with the fruit of his mouth; and with the increase of his lips shall he be filled.

Proverbs 18:20

God's Word says that what you are saying with your mouth is feeding your stomach.

The tongue of the just is as choice silver: the heart of the wicked is little worth. The lips of the righteous feed many.

Proverbs 10:20,21

By confessing prosperity Scriptures for other people and other families, you can stand in proxy faith for others and receive blessings for them.

The law of poverty says:

Love not sleep, lest thou come to poverty; open thine eyes, and thou shalt be satisfied with bread.

Proverbs 20:13

(That cuts you out of sleeping in the morning!)

The sluggard will not plow by reason of the cold; therefore shall he beg in harvest, and have nothing.

Proverbs 20:4

In other words, financial partnership with Jesus rules out laziness!

The law of giving says:

He that hath a bountiful eye shall be blessed; for he giveth of his bread to the poor.

Proverbs 22:9

He that hath pity upon the poor lendeth unto the Lord.

Proverbs 19:17

He that giveth unto the poor shall not lack: but he that hideth his eyes shall have many a curse.

Proverbs 28:27

Giving to the poor will bring prosperity into your own household. It is a sure financial transaction with the Lord! Take God's exciting road and hundredfold blessings will be yours.

Are you ready for a plunge into financial partnership with the Lord Jesus Christ? Bow your head and follow these articles of this partnership prayer:

I acknowledge my need; it is _____.
I turn my gaze from interim sources of prosperity to my total Supplier and close the doors to all unbelief.

Open, dear God, Your door of prosperity. I have the key, Jesus Christ, right in my heart. The grooves of the key (the five activites) *are all precisely etched in my heart to smoothly operate the lock, and I turn the key right now. Amen!*

For all the promises of God in him are yea, and in him Amen, unto the glory of God by us (2 Cor. 1:20).

Endnotes

Chapter 3

1 Based on a definition from James Strong, "Hebrew and Chaldee Dictionary" in *Strong's Exhaustive Concordance of the Bible* (Nashville: Abingdon, 1890), p. 125, entry #8544, s.v. "thy likeness," Psalm 17:15.

2 Ibid, p. 99, entry #6754, s.v. "shew," Psalm 39:6.

3 *International Standard Bible Encyclopedia,* Original James Orr 1915 Edition, Electronic Database. Copyright © 1995-1996 by Biblesoft. All rights reserved, s.v. "AVEN."

4 Based on a definition from Brown, Driver, Briggs and Gesenius, *The KJV Old Testament Hebrew Lexicon,* Hebrew Lexicon entry for "aven," <http://www.biblestudytools.net/Lexicons/Hebrew/heb.cgi?number=0205&version=kjv>, s.v. "0205."

5 *International Standard Bible Encyclopedia,* s.v. "BETH."

6 *New Unger's Bible Dictionary* originally published by Moody Press of Chicago, Illinois. Copyright © 1988. Used by permission, s.v. "BETH-AVEN."

7 Ibid, s.v. "EL."

8 Ibid, s.v. "BETHEL."

⁹ Based on a definition from *The KJV Old Testament Hebrew Lexicon,* Hebrew Lexicon entry for 6089, <http://www.bible studytools.net/Lexicons/Hebrew/heb.cgi?number=6089&version=kjv>, s.v. "labour."

¹⁰ Ibid, Hebrew Lexicon entry for 8251, <http://www.bible studytools.net/Lexicons/Hebrew/heb.cgi?number=8251&version=kjv>, s.v. "Shiqquwts."

Chapter 4

¹ *Jamieson, Fausset and Brown Commentary,* Electronic Database. Copyright © 1997 by Biblesoft. All rights reserved, s.v. "Genesis 41:45."

² *International Standard Bible Encyclopedia,* s.v. "Joseph."

³ Strong, p. 68, entry #4519, s.v. "Genesis 41:51."

⁴ *The KJV Old Testament Hebrew Lexicon,* Hebrew Lexicon entry for 0669, <http://www.biblestudytools.net/Lexicons/Hebrew/ heb.cgi?number=669&version=kjv>, s.v. "Ephraim."

Chapter 7

¹ Based on information from Finis Jennings Dake, *The Dake Annotated Reference Bible,* (Lawrenceville, Georgia: Dake Bible Sales Inc., copyright 1963, 1991), "Genesis 17:1."

About the Author

Marilyn Hickey is no stranger to impacting the lives of millions worldwide. As founder and president of Marilyn Hickey Ministries, Marilyn is being used by God to help "cover the earth with the Word." Her mission has been effectively accomplished through various avenues of ministry such as partnering with other ministries to ship thousands of Bibles into Communist countries; holding crusades in places like Ethiopia, the Philippines, Korea, Haiti, Brazil, Malaysia, Japan, and Honduras; and reaching individuals worldwide through television broadcasts seen on networks such as *Black Entertainment Network* (BET) and *Trinity Broadcasting Network* (TBN). In addition, Marilyn Hickey Ministries has established a fully accredited 2-year Bible college to raise up Christian leaders to carry out God's mission. Marilyn also serves the body of Christ as the Chairman of the Board of Regents for Oral Roberts University, and is the only woman serving on the Board of Directors for Dr. David Yonggi Cho (pastor of the world's largest congregation, Yoido Full Gospel Church.)

In addition to her ministry, Marilyn is also a busy wife and mother of two grown children. She is married to Wallace Hickey, pastor of Orchard Road Christian Center in Greenwood Village, Colorado.

Other Books by Marilyn Hickey

A Cry for Miracles

Angels All Around

Breaking Generational Curses

Breaking Free From Fear

Devils, Demons and Deliverance

God's Covenant for Your Family

…He Will Give You Another Helper

How To Be a Mature Christian

Know Your Ministry

Maximize Your day

Names of God

Release the Power of the Blood Covenant

Satan-Proof Your Home

Signs in the Heavens

When Only a Miracle Will Do

Your Total Health Handbook:
Spirit, Soul and Body

Beat Tension

Bold Men Win

Born-Again and Spirit-Filled

Bull Dog Faith

Change Your Life

Children Who Hit the Mark

Conquering Setbacks

Date To Be An Achiever

Don't Park Here

Experience Long Life

Fasting and Prayer

God's Benefit: Healing

Hold on to Your Dream

How To Win Friends

Keys to Healing Rejection

More Than a Conqueror

Power of Forgiveness

Power of the Blood

Receiving Resurrection Power

Renew Your Mind

Seven Keys to Make You Rich

Solving Life's Problems

Speak the Word

Stand in the Gap

Story of Esther

Tithes, Offerings, Alms

God's Plan for Blessing You!

Winning Over Weight

Women of the Word

RECEIVE JESUS CHRIST
AS LORD AND SAVIOR

The Bible says, "That if thou shalt confess with thy mouth the Lord Jesus, and shalt believe in thine heart that God hath raised him from the dead, thou shalt be saved. For with the heart man believeth unto righteousness; and with the mouth confession is made unto salvation" (Romans 10:9,10).

To receive Jesus Christ as Lord and Savior of your life, sincerely pray this prayer from your heart:

Dear Jesus,

I believe that You died for me and that You rose again on the third day. I confess to You that I am a sinner and that I need Your love and forgiveness. Come into my life, forgive my sins and give me eternal life. I confess You now as my Lord. Thank You for my salvation.

Signed_____ Dated _____

Write to us.
We will send you information to help you
with your new life in Christ.

Marilyn Hickey Ministries · P.O. Box 17340
Denver, CO 80217 · (303) 770-0400

Or visit us on the Web:
www.mhmin.org

Prayer Requests

Let us join our faith with yours for your prayer needs.
Fill out below and send to:

Marilyn Hickey Ministries
P.O. Box 17340
Denver, CO 80217

Prayer request _____

_____

_____

Mr. & Mrs. ☐   Mr. ☐   Miss ☐

Name _____

Address _____

City _____

State_____ Zip _____

Home Phone (_____) _____

Work Phone (_____) _____

Call for prayer TOLL-FREE, 24-hours a day
1-877-661-1249.

Or leave your prayer request
at our website/ministry center:
www.mhmin.org

WORD TO THE WORLD COLLEGE

Explore your options and increase your knowledge of the Word at this unique college of higher learning for men and women of faith. Word to the World College **offers on-campus and correspondence courses** that give you the opportunity to learn from Marilyn Hickey and other great Bible scholars, who can help prepare you to be an effective minister of the gospel. Classes are available for both full- and part-time students.

For more information, complete the coupon below and send to:

Word to the World College
P.O. Box 17340
Denver, CO 80217
(303)770-0400

Mr. & Mrs. ☐   Mr. ☐   Miss ☐

Name _____

Address _____

City _____

State_____ Zip _____

Home Phone (_____) _____

Work Phone (_____) _____

Or contact us on the Web: www.mhmin.org

For Your Information
Free Monthly Magazine

Please send me your free monthly magazine OUT-POURING (including daily devotionals, timely articles, and ministry updates)!

Tapes and Books

Please send me Marilyn's latest product catalog:

Mr. & Mrs. ☐   Mr. ☐   Miss ☐

Name _____

Address _____

City _____

State_____ Zip _____

Home Phone (_____) _____

Work Phone (_____) _____

Mail to:
Marilyn Hickey Ministries
P.O. box 17340
Denver, CO 80217
(303) 770-0400

Additional copies of this book

Are available from your local bookstore.

Harrison House

Tulsa, Oklahoma 74153

The Harrison House Vision

Proclaiming the truth and the power

Of the Gospel of Jesus Christ

With excellence;

Challenging Christians to

Live victoriously,

Grow spiritually,

Know God intimately.